A Note to Parents

DK READERS is a compelling program for beginning readers, designed in conjunction with leading literacy experts, including Dr. Linda Gambrell, Distinguished Professor of Education at Clemson University. Dr. Gambrell has served as President of the National Reading Conference, the College Reading Association, and the International Reading Association.

Beautiful illustrations and superb full-color photographs combine with engaging, easy-to-read stories to offer a fresh approach to each subject in the series. Each DK READER is guaranteed to capture a child's interest while developing his or her reading skills, general knowledge, and love of reading.

The five levels of DK READERS are aimed at different reading abilities, enabling you to choose the books that are exactly right for your child:

Pre-level 1: Learning to read
Level 1: Beginning to read
Level 2: Beginning to read alone
Level 3: Reading alone
Level 4: Proficient readers

The "normal" age at which a child begins to read can be anywhere from three to eight years old. Adult participation through the lower levels is very helpful for providing encouragement, discussing storylines, and sounding out unfamiliar words.

No matter which level you select, you can be sure that you are helping your child learn to read, then read to learn!

DK

LONDON, NEW YORK, MUNICH,
MELBOURNE, AND DELHI

Project Editor Penny Smith
Designer Michelle Baxter
US Editor Regina Kahney
Production Editor Marc Staples
Picture Research Christine Rista
Publishing Manager Bridget Giles
Art Director Martin Wilson
Natural History Consultant
Colin McCarthy

Reading Consultant
Linda B. Gambrell, Ph.D.

First American Edition, 1998
This edition, 2011
16 15 14 13 12 11 10
Published in the United States by DK Publishing
345 Hudson Street, New York, New York 10014
010-KP811-Jun/2011
Copyright © 1998 Dorling Kindersley Limited

Published in Great Britain by Dorling Kindersley Limited.

DK books are available at special discounts when purchased in bulk
for sales promotions, premiums, fund-raising, or educational use.
For details, contact: DK Publishing Special Markets
345 Hudson Street, New York, New York 10014
SpecialSales@dk.com

A catalog record for this book is available
from the Library of Congress

ISBN: 978-0-7566-7587-5 (pb)
ISBN: 978-0-7566-7588-2 (plc)

Color reproduction by Colourscan, Singapore
Printed and bound in L.Rex Printing Co.Ltd

The publisher would like to thank the following for their kind
permission to reproduce their photographs:
a=above; c=center; b=below/bottom; l=left; r=right; t=top

Bruce Coleman Ltd: Gunter Ziesler 26–27; John Cancalosi 28; John
Visser 22, 23t; MPL Fogden 21cl; Rod Williams 16–17; **N.H.P.A.:**
Anthony Bannister 24b; Daniel Heuclin 18, 29t; KH Switak 14;
Oxford Scientific Films: Alastair Shay 3, 20; **Planet Earth Pictures:**
Brian Kenney 12; **Warren Photographic:** Jane Burton 9b **Jacket
images:** *Front:* **Getty Images:** Stone / Kevin Horan.

All other images © Dorling Kindersley.
For further information see: www.dkimages.com

Discover more at
www.dk.com

DK READERS

BEGINNING TO READ ALONE 2

Slinky, Scaly Snakes!

Written by Jennifer Dussling

DK Publishing

Slinky, scaly snakes
slide along the ground.

They have legless bodies
and look through unblinking eyes.

Everglades rat snake

Snakes are shiny
and can look slimy.
But they are dry
and smooth to touch.

Rattlesnake

A snake's whole body
s covered in scales.
These scales are hard and tough
ike fingernails.

Snakes grow quickly,
but their skin doesn't stretch.
When a snake's skin gets too tight,
the snake has to shed it.
This is called molting.

Rock python

The snake rubs its head
on something rough like a log.
After a few minutes,
the skin begins to peel.

*The shed skin
of a snake*

The snake slides forward
and right out of its skin!
Underneath is a new skin.
It looks bright and shiny.
The snake keeps on growing.
Soon it will be time
to molt again.

Wait and see
When a snake is ready
to molt, its eyes turn
milky white. The snake
is almost blind for a week,
so it stays hidden.

Snakes have no legs.
They move in long, slinky curves.
The ground may look smooth
but it has little bumps everywhere.
A snake pushes off the bumps
to move itself forward.

The sidewinder snake
lives in the desert.
It throws itself forward
one part at a time.
It leaves behind
wavy-looking tracks.

Eyelash viper

Not all snakes live on the ground.

Some live in trees.

Long-lost legs

Millions of years ago, snakes had legs like lizards. The closest relative of snakes today is thought to be the monitor lizard.

Snakes may not have legs, but they can still climb. A snake has scales on its belly that are larger than the ones on its back. These scales grip the tree. The snake uses its strong muscles to pull itself up the tree.

Boa constrictor

How are snakes born?
Some give birth to live babies.
Other snakes lay eggs.

Florida kingsnake laying eggs

Soft shell
Snake eggs
are not hard
like chicken eggs.
The shells are soft,
almost like leather.

A mother snake doesn't usually stay with her eggs.

She lays them in a soft, warm place, then she leaves them.

Soon a baby snake pokes its head out of the egg.

Then it slithers out of its shell.

Rat snake

Haitian (HAY-shun) boa

This snake is not moving.

Only its tongue flicks in and out.

It is checking for danger.

Most snakes can't see or hear well.
But they have
a strong sense of smell.
And they pick up these smells
with their tongues.

A fox meets a whipsnake

But what are snakes afraid of?
Hawks, raccoons, and foxes
like to eat snakes.
Some snakes eat other snakes.
But many snakes have ways
to fool their enemies.

Some snakes blend in
with the area around them.
This vine snake looks like
a vine hanging from a tree.

These gaboon vipers
look like fallen leaves.

Other snakes try to trick
their enemies.

The parrot snake
opens its mouth very wide
and tries to look scary.

The milk snake is harmless.
But it looks like
the deadly coral snake,
so animals stay away.

Coral snake

Milk snake

The grass snake has a great trick.
When an enemy is near,
it plays dead!

All snakes are meat-eaters.
Small snakes eat small animals
like bugs, lizards, and worms.
Some snakes eat eggs.
This snake is swallowing a bird's egg.

Egg-eating snake

The egg makes a big bulge
in the snake's body.

The egg breaks inside the snake.
Then the snake spits out the shell.

A rat makes a tasty meal
for a boa constrictor.

First the snake grabs the rat.
The snake holds on fast
with its strong jaws.

Tight squeeze
Snakes crush their prey,
but they don't break bones.
They squeeze just enough
to make the animal
stop breathing.

It wraps its long body
around and around the rat.
Then the snake starts to squeeze
tight … tighter … tighter.
Soon the rat's heart stops.

The snake opens its mouth
very, very wide.
It gulps once or twice
and swallows the rat headfirst.

A rock python swallowing a Thomson's gazelle

Big snakes eat bigger animals.
Giant pythons and boas
can be as long as a school bus.
They eat pigs, goats, and gazelles.

Big eaters

A meal can last
a long time.
Snakes like this python
have gone a whole year
without eating!

Mojave rattlesnake

Many snakes use poison
to kill their food.
The poison is stored in sacs
close to their long, sharp fangs.

The snake sticks its fangs
into the animal.

*Uracoan
rattlesnake*

The poison shoots through the
fangs and into the animal's body.
It does not take long
for the animal to die.
Then the snake swallows it whole.

Born to kill

A cobra can kill from
the minute it is born.
Just one tablespoon
of its dried poison
can kill 160,000 mice!

Can snakes hurt people?

Many can.

Here are some snakes
that can poison people.

Rattlesnake

Copperhead

Cobra

But if people are bitten,

snakes can help!

Medicine is made from their poison

to treat snake bites.

Biting people better
A snake bites through
the thin covering
over a container.
Poison dripping from
its fangs is collected.

Snakes are useful in lots of ways.

They eat millions of mice

and other pests.

And they are eaten

by other hungry animals.

Our world would not be the same

without slinky, scaly snakes!

Snake facts

Snakes are cold-blooded.
They lie in the sun to warm up
and move into the shade
to cool down.

Unlike people,
snakes never stop growing.

The world's heaviest snake
is the anaconda.
It can weigh as much
as three grown men.

The smallest snake
is the thread snake.
It is as skinny
as the lead in a pencil!

Baby snakes have a tooth
to help them break their eggs.
It falls off soon after they hatch.

It's not hard
to outrun a snake.
The fastest ones slither
at the same speed as you walk.